Old Sarum

John McNeill

Introduction

Old Sarum is one of the most enthralling historic sites in southern England. Uniquely, it combines evidence for a royal castle and cathedral within a massive Iron Age fortification. During the century and a half when its castle and cathedral coexisted, Old Sarum was a major centre of government.

The earliest fortification was probably raised around 400 BC. Following the arrival of the Romans, Old Sarum begins to feature in recorded history as Sorviodunum, and it was intermittently occupied during the early Middle Ages, when its formidable defences became an advantage during the Danish wars of the early 11th century.

However, it was William the Conqueror's decision in about 1070 to build a royal castle in the middle of the old earthworks that was to transform the site. He effectively divided the old hillfort in two, creating an inner set of fortifications which became home to a complex of towers, halls and apartments, and a huge outer enclosure or bailey. The hillfort was also chosen as the site for a new cathedral, and under Old Sarum's most powerful and influential bishop, Roger (1102–39), both castle and cathedral were rebuilt on a grand scale.

Yet neither castle nor cathedral remained occupied for long. In 1220 the cathedral was moved to Salisbury, in the valley below, and only a handful of people continued to live within the castle or ramparts beyond about 1400. Old Sarum lived on, however, and as a notorious 'rotten borough' it continued to elect members of Parliament until 1832.

Above: Two lions grasping the top of a small gable. This is one of the most famous fragments of sculpture from the early 12th-century cathedral excavated at Old Sarum in the early 20th century. The surviving stonework suggests that the cathedral was one of the most extravagant buildings of its day in England

Facing page: The courtyard house in the inner bailey, probably built by Bishop Roger, with the keep beyond

The Tour

There are three major points of interest to visit at Old Sarum: the earthworks of the Iron Age hillfort, the inner stronghold of the Norman castle on the mound at the centre of the site, and the remains of the cathedral, within the north-west quarter of the hillfort.

FOLLOWING THE TOUR

The tour begins just inside the medieval castle, and follows a suggested route around the castle buildings before exploring the outer bailey, cathedral and finally the Iron Age ramparts. The numbers beside the headings highlight key points on the tour and correspond with the small numbered plans in the margins.

THE MEDIEVAL CASTLE

The present approach to Old Sarum follows, in its final stages, the route which most visitors have taken from the late Iron Age onwards. The narrow track from the main road twists through a gap in the ramparts where the castle's east gate stood, and into the outer bailey of the medieval castle, now an area of open grassland. The car park lies inside this entrance.

From here, the inner bailey of the medieval castle is approached over a modern wooden bridge, bringing you through the former gatehouse. The earthworks supporting the various buildings which make up the castle around you were created shortly after the Norman Conquest. The freshly dug chalk would have needed time to settle, and the royal castle first mentioned in about 1070 is likely to have been of timber. The stone structures which replaced this came into being piecemeal during the 12th and early 13th centuries.

Walk a short way into the inner bailey. Ahead of you are the remains of the keep and postern tower, while to the right there was a palatial residence now known as the courtyard house. If you were standing here in 1250 you would also have seen a large rectangular hall with adjacent kitchen and bakery over to the left. You would also have felt appreciably more protected, as the banks around the inner bailey supported a stone wall with battlements.

The castle walls mainly survive as rough flint cores which were once covered with smooth facing stone. After the site was excavated in 1909–12, it was sometimes necessary to replace facing stone, and if so, the date was added – hence you will see the occasional stone inscribed 1910 or 1912.

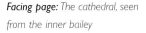

Facing page: The cathedral, seen from the inner bailey

Below: Old Sarum looking north-east. The earthworks of the Iron Age ramparts (the outer ring) and the motte of the medieval castle (the inner ring) show up very clearly against the snow. The plan of the cathedral is just visible on the left

Above: The courtyard house as it might have looked in the late 12th century, with the gatehouse beyond. The west range, shown cut away in the foreground, acted as the hall. Evidence for the green crested ridge tiles and elaborate chimneys was found in the 1910 excavations, though the precise height of the four main ranges is a matter of conjecture

◼ COURTYARD HOUSE

This is the most ambitious structure inside the inner bailey; it is also the least well understood. It was probably built by Roger of Sarum, Old Sarum's third and most prominent bishop, who had custody of the castle (as well as the cathedral) between about 1130 and 1139. The link with Roger is likely, because the palace is so similar in plan to Sherborne Old Castle, Dorset, which he is known to have built. Although we cannot be certain of its precise internal arrangements, the courtyard house seems to have contained a hall, chamber block, kitchen and service wing, and a chapel arranged over two storeys. The integration of these elements in a single building at this date is usually only seen in the very grandest keeps, such as Rochester or the Tower of London, but here is organised as four ranges of buildings around a small courtyard.

This arrangement is best seen from the path up from the gatehouse, where it is clear that the courtyard – visible behind the green railings – is about 4.6m (15ft) above the level of the inner bailey. The house was in fact built on two levels, and the south and east ranges (those nearest to you) had to be planned with lower storeys. From this same position you can also see that the exterior wall was set on a stone base or plinth and supported at regular intervals with buttresses.

The east range (to your right) seems to have been a service range, and the kitchen tower and associated cesspits can be seen rising up the bank beyond. If you go inside, you can see that the lower room was divided into three parts in the 14th century: judging by the remains of what must have been a magnificent fireplace on the right (east) wall (the projecting back of the flue is clear from outside), this was originally a very grand guardroom. A spiral staircase to the north gave access to the upper floor.

Return to the inner bailey and walk around past the well to the south range of the house. This contained a two-storey chapel: the upper storey is thought to have been dedicated to St Nicholas and the lower storey to St Margaret. An opening close to the middle of the south range takes you down into the chapel of St Margaret. A masonry bench survives along the south wall, and the projecting spurs of flint visible here are the remains of bases for 12th-century pilasters or half-columns. There is no evidence for a corresponding bench on the north wall. The altar base has been reconstructed at the east end, which was originally surmounted by a barrel vault (where the wall narrows). This lower chapel would have been for the castle garrison, with the larger chapel of St Nicholas above reserved for the royal household or its representatives.

The western end of the south range consists of three rooms, all of which show evidence of extensive later medieval alteration. We do not know what any of these spaces were used for, although the westernmost is likely to have housed the stairway which brought visitors up from the inner bailey to the hall.

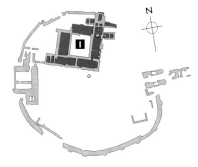

Below: The chapel of St Margaret, in the south range of the courtyard house. The altar base is visible on the far (east) wall

Bottom: The courtyard house seen from the south, looking across the inner bailey

Roger of Sarum

As one of Henry I's closest advisers, after 1120 Roger was made regent, governing during Henry's absences abroad

Above: Sherborne Old Castle, built by Roger of Sarum

Below: It was while Roger was chancellor that the office of the exchequer (so called after a method of audit that used counters on a chequer board) came into being. This illustration from a 12th-century manuscript shows officials receiving and weighing coin

Roger of Sarum was a priest from Avranches in south-west Normandy, who entered service with the future Henry I as a chaplain. In 1101, shortly after he became king, Henry appointed Roger as his chancellor, and the chapter at Old Sarum Cathedral elected him bishop the following year.

Until Henry I's death in 1135, Roger was one of his closest advisers, radically reorganising the royal finances and record-keeping. After 1120 Roger was made regent, governing during Henry's absences abroad. According to the monk-chronicler William of Malmesbury, he dealt with his ecclesiastical responsibilities in the morning, 'so that he could speedily and safely proceed to other things'. Contemporaries also remarked on the pride he took in his buildings – 'a pride unsurpassed within the recollection of our age'. In addition to his work at Old Sarum, Roger had castles built at Kidwelly (Wales), Sherborne in Dorset, and Malmesbury and Devizes, Wiltshire; the last was described by Henry of Huntingdon as 'the most splendid castle in Europe'. His patronage extended to his family: two of his nephews rose through the chapter of Old Sarum to become bishops (Alexander at Lincoln and Nigel at Ely), while his son by his mistress was briefly chancellor to King Stephen.

Roger's downfall came in the summer of 1139 when he was summoned, with his nephews, to attend the new king, Stephen, at Oxford. The three were arrested following a contrived brawl and Roger was forced to forfeit his castles. He was later released but died on 11 December at Old Sarum. Roger's reputation as a brilliant and innovative administrator and bishop seems to have deserted him in later life, and William of Malmesbury concluded his obituary: 'While to many he seemed a man of sorrows, yet very few were sorry for him'.

To reach the upper ranges of the house you should climb the slope at the far end of the south range. The west range, marked out in the grass to the right, was probably the site of the hall – the most public room of the house, where visitors would be received. The only grand feature of the hall to survive – the base of a doorway from the courtyard – would not have been the public entrance. Visitors would originally have arrived via a stairway housed at the west end of the south range.

The tiny courtyard, now set as lawn, would originally have felt rather like an enclosed cloister, though with wooden covered walks on the north and west sides only. The north range, to your left, was probably for the use of the castle's principal occupant, and would have housed the bedchamber. There are remains of a fireplace in the north wall – stones belonging to its elaborate 12th-century chimney were discovered in 1910. The deep latrine pits visible behind the railings to the north are later additions, and were probably set beneath rooms reached from the main range, rather like private bathrooms. The range is described in a later account as accommodating the 'great chamber by Herlewin's Tower'.

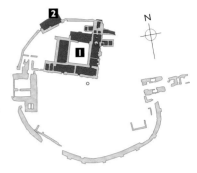

▣ HERLEWIN'S TOWER

Herlewin's Tower lies just north-west of the courtyard house, right above the inner bailey ditch, and is represented by the low rectangular wall cutting across the corner of the bank here. It seems to have been built specifically to look out over the cathedral, probably shortly after the courtyard house was erected but before the building of the curtain wall in 1172–3; the wall simply butts up against it. You can also see, to the right of the tower and behind railings, the base of steps which belong to the curtain wall and originally led up to the sentry walk. Now, as then, this spot offers a stunning view over the old cathedral quarter.

Below: The latrine pits which served the north range of the courtyard house

THE COURTYARD HOUSE, LOOKING SOUTH-WEST

1 Courtyard

2 East range (guardroom)

3 South range (chapels)

4 West range (hall)

5 North range ('great chamber')

6 Kitchen cesspits

🔳 🔳 KEEP AND POSTERN TOWER

Walk back down the slope towards the keep. Closing the west side of the inner bailey, this originally took the form of a massive stone tower. On the far (south) side is a small annexe, while the passage to the north originally ran to a postern or back gate. As the centrepiece of the castle, the keep was designed to impress, and was tellingly placed opposite the main entrance. Seen from the bailey, its most striking feature today is a sloping base, with facing stone that runs continuously into the southern annexe. The keep was clearly in existence by 1130, when the sheriff of Wiltshire spent 20 shillings on making an entrance into the cellar of the tower, and building may have begun as early as about 1100.

The present entry to the keep is from the postern passage, via steps through a ragged post-medieval breach in its north wall. This leads you up into a pair of rooms divided by a cross wall. Both these rooms were probably used for storage – the important rooms would have been above you. From the furthest room there is a good view of the stepped plinth with which the west face of the southern annexe is so boldly finished.

Return to the passageway to the north of the keep. When the keep was built, this led to the postern gate of the castle, but it was later blocked in two places. There are drawbar holes at both ends of the south wall of the passage, showing that the guards could shut both the inner and outer passage doors; these must be broadly contemporary with the building of the keep. A tower is mentioned as existing above the passage in 1246, but it is likely that the postern tower was erected, and the passageway blocked, considerably earlier than this. The blocking walls were probably built in the late 12th or early 13th century, when it became necessary to build a new route from the postern gate to the inner bailey.

This later route into the castle can still be traced by going up the modern steps opposite the present entrance to the keep, and turning left down the slope. On your right as you come back up you pass the gatekeeper's niche — a sort of masonry sentry-box. As you continue up and turn right, you pass the beginnings of a flight of steps which turns back over the postern passage. These steps are impossible to date precisely, but they would have formed the only way into the postern tower, and also the principal entrance to the keep beyond, on an upper floor. To return to the inner bailey, turn right again in front of the courtyard house.

Go round the keep to view the small annexe on its south side. It has been suggested that this building was a treasury, on the basis of a document of 1181–2, which tells us that £9 1s 0d was spent constructing a treasury in the keep. However, not only is the sum of money involved too small to cover the cost of building such an annexe, but its facing masonry is continuous with that of the main keep, which suggests that it was built at the same time, rather than later. Sherborne and Corfe castles, built at a similar date, also have rectangular keeps with integral annexes. At Corfe, the annexe contained a guardroom, chapel and privy, and it is possible that the same was true here. All that now survives in the southern annexe (which is not accessible to visitors) is a cesspit for the latrine and a cross-arch supporting the first floor.

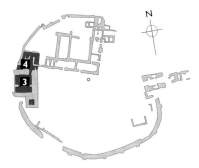

Above: The flight of steps that once led up into the postern tower and formed the principal entrance to the keep

Left: The keep as it may have looked in the late 12th century, before the postern passage was blocked. Keeps of this date were always entered at first-floor level, with the stairs either enclosed within a forebuilding, or constructed from wood. The original access at Old Sarum may have been via a wooden staircase on the east (left) face; this was then replaced by the stone steps shown here, which brought visitors in on the north face, when the postern tower was built. Alternatively, the access may always have been on the north side, and the present stairs may simply replicate an earlier arrangement

5 6 NEW HALL AND KITCHEN/BAKEHOUSE

Although the courtyard house and keep were the most important buildings within the inner bailey, evidence for a number of other structures was unearthed during excavations in 1910–12. To the left of the keep are sections of a long stone wall bench that belongs to a rectangular hall; at the end nearest the keep is the base of a smart doorway. This presumably gave onto a little courtyard or garden by the southern annexe to the keep. The public entrance to this hall was probably along its long side facing the bailey, with a service entrance at the east end. Built between 1201 and 1208, during the reign of King John, the hall features in a list of buildings in need of repair in 1247, where it is described as the new hall. It would have been used for court hearings by the sheriff of Wiltshire, the king's officer in the county, and was probably also the hall used on a day-to-day basis by the resident castle garrison.

The section of rampart just behind the hall has the twin advantages of providing the best views of Salisbury – the cathedral spire is the most visible landmark – and of revealing the terrific depth of the inner bailey ditch. You can either climb the bank here or use the steps nearer the gatehouse.

If you walk along the top of this rampart towards the ticket office, you can look down on the base of a T-shaped building with three rooms. The largest of these contained three bread ovens. These are the only surviving remains of a kitchen and bakehouse built to replace an earlier kitchen by the new hall, which collapsed in 1307.

At the south-east angle by the gatehouse is the one section of masonry wall that still stands above the old earthen

Above: A baker placing loaves in an oven, from a manuscript of about 1340. A new bakehouse and kitchen were built at Old Sarum in the early 14th century
Below: The view from the ramparts looking south towards Salisbury – the cathedral is visible in the centre, with Clearbury Ring, another Iron Age hillfort, on the horizon beyond the spire

rampart. When the inner bailey was first created under William the Conqueror, the tops of its ramparts would have carried a simple timber palisade. This was replaced in 1172–3 by a stone curtain wall. It seems that this improvement to the castle's defences had not been anticipated when the gatehouse was revamped some two years earlier, and it was probably a hasty response to the great crisis of Henry II's reign in 1173, when his wife, children and many of his barons rebelled against him (see page 29).

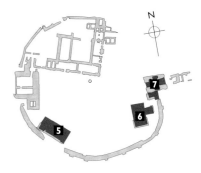

7 GATEHOUSE

Walk back past the ticket office. As you go through the gatehouse passage, you pass first through a narrow western section of the gatehouse which could be closed by an inner set of doors. Beyond, there are vaulted guardrooms on either side of the passage. On your right, just before you cross the bridge, is the drawbar slot for the outer doors.

The clearest view of the outer face of the gatehouse is from the far side of the castle ditch – which would have been dry, not filled with water. Here you can see how the forward faces of the buttresses marking the entrance have fallen away. Beneath these are the remains of earlier bridge supports and the drawbridge pit. The gatehouse would originally have been approached over a wooden drawbridge which hinged on a pivot, like a see-saw with one end shorter than the other. The surviving masonry of the gatehouse is comparable to that of the courtyard house, suggesting that it too was probably built in the 1130s. It was refurbished by Henry II in 1170–71, when money was spent on the bridge, and again in the 1240s.

Left: The castle ditch, looking towards the modern bridge

The Oath of Sarum

The Oath of Sarum was both an act of great political theatre – an assertion of William's right to the loyalty of his subjects – and an administrative exercise

According to the Anglo-Saxon Chronicle, on Lammas Day (1 August) 1086, William the Conqueror came to Old Sarum 'and his council came to him, and all the landholding men of any account throughout England, whosoever's men they were, and they all bowed down to him and became his men, and swore oaths of fealty to him that they would be faithful to him against all other men'.

Historians attach great importance to this event. It means that William insisted that the allegiance owed by landholders to him took precedence over their loyalty to their immediate overlord or, if they held French lands, the king of France. From then on, if one of the magnates of the realm were to take up arms against the Crown, the first loyalty of his sub-tenants would be to the English king.

What the landholders got in return is uncertain, but by the summer of 1086 the survey of landholding on which Domesday Book was based had probably been completed, and it could be that the oaths secured the estates of William's tenants-in-chief and their under-tenants. In other words, the Oath of Sarum was both an act of great political theatre – an assertion of William's right to the loyalty of his subjects – and an administrative exercise – an affirmation of the post-Conquest patterns of landholding enshrined in Domesday. Old Sarum was probably chosen to host the assembly because it was the administrative base from which the Domesday survey of the south-western counties was conducted.

Right: A 14th-century depiction of William the Conqueror on horseback, wearing the arms of England and accompanied by knights and soldiers

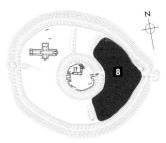

8 OUTER BAILEY

When the castle and inner bailey were first created around 1070, two banks, connecting the inner bailey with the outer ramparts, were erected to divide the remainder of the old hillfort into unequal halves. The eastern portion formed the outer bailey of the castle. If you turn left after crossing the bridge and walk anticlockwise, you will see one of these tree-covered banks to your right.

Little is known about the use of the outer bailey at Old Sarum, though normally such areas housed castle service buildings, as well as accommodating lavish open-air ceremonial. What has become known as the Oath of Sarum would almost certainly have taken place here (see feature opposite).

The underlying ground of the outer bailey shelves downwards from the inner castle towards the former east gate of the hillfort, an incline which would have appeared steeper before the spoil from the 1909–12 castle excavations – up to 4.6m (15ft) thick in places – was spread out in the area now occupied by the car park. The surrounding hillfort ramparts would initially have been topped by a timber palisade, which was subsequently replaced to the south by a masonry wall.

There is now relatively little to see in the outer bailey. Its most striking physical feature is a large crater beneath the north bank, visible before you reach the radial bank. This was caused by the partial collapse of a tunnel, excavated in 1957 and seemingly medieval. It originally ran beneath the ramparts, and was perhaps intended as a sallyport, or side entrance, connecting the castle with Salisbury plain to the north.

To reach the cathedral, which occupies the north-west quarter of the old hillfort, continue walking anticlockwise from the gatehouse.

Above: One of the radial banks connecting the inner bailey ditch with the outer ramparts, and acting as the eastern boundary of the cathedral precinct

Below: Drawings from the Gentleman's Magazine *in 1795, illustrating the newly discovered tunnel beneath the ramparts. The tunnel was excavated in 1957 (see page 39)*

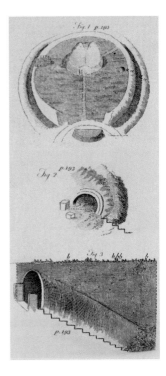

9 CATHEDRAL PRECINCT

After the site of the cathedral was excavated between 1912 and 1915, upstanding masonry was left visible, and the cathedral foundations were marked out in the grass. Most of the building materials had already been removed after the cathedral was transferred to Salisbury, and superficially it looks as if the site has been picked almost clean. However, more than is now visible was revealed in the excavations. Much of this – the best of the Romanesque sculpture, for instance – was found heaped in storage pits. Some, such as the evidence for the bishop's palace, has simply been covered back over.

A good place to view the entire precinct is from the centre of the church (where there is an information panel). Facing west from here, you are looking down the nave of the first cathedral, begun under Bishop Herman (1045–78) about 1075 and consecrated in 1092 under Bishop Osmund (1078–99). The bases of the piers in the crossing, along with the transepts (side arms) and massively extended presbytery behind you, belong to an enlargement of the cathedral undertaken while Roger of Sarum was bishop (1102–39). To the north-east, at a lower level, you can make out the four walks of an irregular cloister. The bishop's palace, first developed under Herman or Osmund, lay beyond this.

10 THE EARLY CATHEDRAL

The first cathedral at Old Sarum was tiny – appreciably smaller than any of the other post-Conquest cathedrals – with a three-apsed east end, narrow transepts with chapels, and a conventional crossing. The foundations of the apses are visible within the outline of the later cathedral. The crossing must have supported the tower, which according to William of Malmesbury was damaged by a violent thunderstorm on 10 April 1092, five days after the consecration of the cathedral.

A platform within the central apse, no longer visible but uncovered during excavation, must have been either for an altar or a bishop's throne; the eastern aisles would have been separated from the presbytery by solid walls or an open arcade. In the nave – the part of the church used by the laity – the piers were cross-shaped, and the aisle walls seem to have been smooth, with neither internal half-columns nor external buttresses. It is most unlikely that the nave was particularly tall, or that its slender walls could have supported galleries.

From its ground plan, the first cathedral seems to have been like a small version of La Trinité at Caen, a church begun shortly before 1066 as a mausoleum for Mathilda, the wife of William the Conqueror, and quite unlike anything else of its date in England. It was probably intended to have a substantial west front with towers, though the foundations you now see belong to a twin-towered west front built later, under Bishop Jocelyn (1142–84).

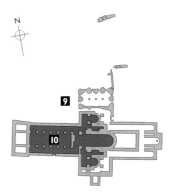

Facing page: The nave of the first cathedral, as it might have looked around 1100. The only aspect of the early cathedral that is known for certain is its footprint – the rest of the reconstruction is based on its similarity to the plan of the church of La Trinité at Caen in Normandy

Below: The aisle of La Trinité (the Abbaye aux Dames) at Caen. The aisle wall is sheer, unbroken by any vertical features

Above: Detail of a piece of decorative stonework discovered in 1912 and believed to be from the choir of Roger's cathedral. Similar designs can be seen in Salisbury Cathedral close wall, where stones from Old Sarum were re-used (see page 35)

THE CATHEDRAL PRECINCT

1 Apse of first cathedral

2 Nave

3 West front

4 Extended presbytery

5 Vestry–treasury

6 Cloister

7 Site of bishop's palace

1 ROGER'S CATHEDRAL

The cathedral inherited by Bishop Roger was unusually modest – a mere 56m (185ft) from apse to west end – and it is likely that he intended to replace it completely. In the event, he built new transepts, a choir and a presbytery, together with a vestry–treasury building just out of sight to the north (see below). The building campaign probably began with the vestry–treasury and proceeded clockwise as far as the south transept and crossing. At this point work stopped. If you look west again from the crossing, it is apparent that the four massive crossing piers of Roger's cathedral were set outside the line of the earlier nave arcade, making for an extremely awkward junction. In other words, the crossing was built on the understanding that the nave would be demolished. That this did not happen suggests that work stopped at this point as the result of Roger's death in 1139. The west front must have been planned after it was decided to retain the nave, under Roger's successor, Jocelyn.

West of the crossing is the base of the pulpitum, the screen which separated the ritual choir from the nave. The choir extended under the crossing as far as the eastern crossing piers, and would also have been fitted out under Jocelyn, probably shortly after 1142. As the area north of the cathedral was occupied by the bishop's palace, the principal entrance for the laity was via a porch attached to the south transept. It was in the area outside this that the greatest concentration of Romanesque sculpture was discovered. The south transept and porch would have been a great show front which could easily be viewed from the castle.

East of the crossing is a presbytery, whose piers were originally set on a low wall separating the central area from the aisles. Three tombs stood on the wall, of Bishop Osmund in the north-east bay, and Roger and Jocelyn to the south. To the east are an ambulatory or walkway and a set of chapels. The chapels at the aisle ends are relatively self-contained, but the peculiar central space, apparently a room flanked by narrow corridors, was probably built as a single chapel with narrow aisles – as at the present Salisbury Cathedral – and was embellished with a magnificent pavement set with porphyry and green marble. It was almost certainly refurbished for the transfer of Bishop Osmund's remains into a type of tomb-shrine in the 1170s. In Roger's time the presbytery and choir were paved with alternating cream and green flagstones.

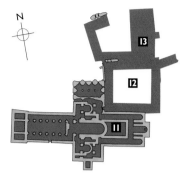

Modern steps lead north from the north transept into what would have been a huge basement room, divided in two by a central row of circular piers. The deep openings visible around the walls are narrow windows; originally the only entrance into the room was via steps beneath the present staircase. Given its position, and the thickness of the walls, this must have been a two-storey building. The upper chamber was reached from the west aisle of the north transept via another set of steps. The building probably housed a treasury on the upper floor, with a vestry-cum-sacristy, for storing some of the liturgical vessels and vestments, below.

Return to the north transept and take the steps on the left, which lead down into the former cloister. A beautifully preserved section of external walling survives to your left, running from the east wall of the vestry–treasury building to the north transept entrance. It is the one place on site where it is possible to get a feel for the exquisite finish of Roger's cathedral.

12 13 CLOISTER AND BISHOP'S PALACE

The cloister itself seems to have been an afterthought. The steps from the north transept were inserted into earlier masonry, and the cloister's eccentric shape suggests that it had to be squeezed in between the cathedral and bishop's palace which had already been built to the south and north. The cloister is likely to have been created in the third quarter of the 12th century, under Bishop Jocelyn.

Sadly, there is no longer anything to be seen of the bishop's palace, which lay beyond the north cloister walk. Archaeologists discovered evidence for two phases of work, the second of which had an aisled hall and ancillary ranges arranged around a courtyard, like the great Wolvesey Palace (in Winchester) of the bishops of Winchester. Old Sarum was almost certainly the earliest bishop's palace of this kind, predating Roger's cathedral extension and built either early in his term of office, or late in Osmund's.

Below: This photograph of the south transept under excavation in 1913 shows the impressions left by the rich pavement in its mortar bedding: deposits in the bed revealed that the stones were of creamy limestone alternating with green sandstone

Above: Old Sarum viewed from the south-west, with some of the buildings of Stratford-sub-Castle in the foreground
Below: A section of the Iron Age bank and ditch along the south-west face of the ramparts, near the west gate

🄸 OUTER RAMPARTS

Although the outer ramparts are the most impressive feature to survive at Old Sarum, relatively little is known about them. The best estimate as to how and when they were built comes from two limited excavations in 1914 and 1957.

If you climb to the top of the bank to the north of the cathedral you can see that the ramparts broadly consist of two earth banks separated by a ditch. In order to create these banks it was only necessary to excavate a single ditch, piling up the spoil to either side. As Old Sarum is a natural mound, and the underlying chalk falls away from the centre outwards, this central ditch did not have to be particularly deep to create impressively steep banks. The archaeology suggests that the ramparts were first created in the early or middle Iron Age, perhaps about 400 BC, and the inner bank was then heightened in either the late Iron Age or early Roman period.

Following the Norman Conquest, the banks were again reinforced when the inner ditch was deepened. Finally, after Roger of Sarum obtained custody of the castle in the 1130s, a masonry curtain wall was built above the inner rampart. A small section of curtain walling survives just north of the cathedral: there are two deep slots on its outer face from which beams would have projected to support a wooden gallery. Although the character of the masonry suggests that this length of wall belongs to a 14th-century repair, it perpetuates the line of Roger's curtain wall. For reasons that remain mysterious, Roger's wall was never completed, and the section of the outer bailey between the north-east radial bank and the east gate had only a timber palisade.

The best way to see the ramparts as a whole is to walk anticlockwise from the cathedral and then follow the rough path to the right, which leads to the former west gate of the medieval castle. The west gate was never much more than a postern – a simple opening in the bank with a threshold and door, but without an elaborate tower above. No evidence was

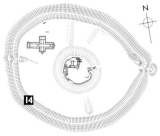

discovered of an Iron Age or Roman opening in the vicinity
and it may be that a west entrance was developed only in the
Middle Ages, presumably in conjunction with the cathedral.

*Below: A section of the Iron Age
bank and ditch near the east gate*

A causeway leads across the ditch here and onto the
outer bank. If you turn left, you can follow the outer bank
round as far as the east gate. At the point where you meet
the metalled road, the earth ramparts survive in depth, with
the remnants of an Iron Age mound or hornwork to your
right: this stood in front of the former east gate (which lies
to your left) and forced any visitor to approach the gate
obliquely. The east gate of the medieval castle would have
been much more impressive than the west entrance and
more like the castle gatehouse, with inner and outer doors.
It is known to have housed an upper chapel dedicated to
the Holy Cross.

The area outside the gate formed a sort of medieval
suburb: medieval chalk quarries, lime kilns and over 70 graves
have been found nearby. If you take the fenced footpath to
the right of the mound at the sharp bend in the entrance
lane, and turn right at the open field, you reach a hollow way,
with trees almost meeting overhead. This was the main street
of the medieval settlement, on the line of the Roman road to
Dorchester. The 'Parliament Tree' stood nearby (see page 37).

From here, retrace your steps to the inner bailey. The toilet
block beyond the car park was built over a Second World
War wireless control room and pillbox, three anti-aircraft guns
having been mounted on the ramparts to protect the airfield
just to the north-east. From the top of the steps here, you
can make out the line of the old Roman road to Winchester
(the modern road to Ford), going up the hill directly opposite.
You can also appreciate another reason for Old Sarum's
position: it stands on a promontory which is connected by a
low neck of land to Bishopdown. From this point it is also
possible to complete a circuit of the ramparts at the higher
level. The whole circular route is about one mile.

History

The history of this windswept hilltop spans thousands of years: within the protective enclosure of the Iron Age ramparts, successive occupants have left their mark. As the site of both a Norman castle and a cathedral, for about 150 years Old Sarum was an important centre of both secular and ecclesiastical government.

READING THE HISTORY

This section describes Old Sarum's prehistoric origins, how and why it was altered at different times, why it was abandoned, and how it was unearthed again. There are special features on the demolition of the cathedral and on the 1957 excavations (see pages 35 and 39).

THE IRON AGE HILLFORT

The key to understanding Old Sarum's early history is its position, for the earthworks rise above the westernmost spur of a ridge – Bishopdown – which separates the rivers Avon and Bourne. To its south, the River Avon picks up the waters of the Nadder, Bourne and Ebble in close succession, and the valley broadens into an extensive flood plain. Old Sarum is one of a number of fortified sites which look out over this expanding valley, including Figsbury Ring and Clearbury Ring. Although there is no reason to suppose these sites developed together, the similarity in their underlying topography is striking.

The date at which the first hillfort was created is difficult to establish, in part because the medieval redevelopment of Old Sarum has obscured the earlier layouts. However, although we cannot be certain how the central area was arranged, the basic form of the hillfort seems reasonably clear. The enclosure is defined by an outer rampart which exploits the underlying shape of the land, so that the height and angle of the banks simply exaggerate the natural scarp of the promontory. This outer rampart encloses an area of approximately 72ha (29 acres) – larger than the vast majority of Iron Age hillforts, but still only just over half the size of the greatest of them, at Maiden Castle in Dorset.

When archaeologists excavated sections of the ramparts in 1957, they discovered evidence for an original entrance facing north, which was blocked before the Roman period. After this, the only entrance was where it is now, on the east side, protected by a ditch and a type of outer bank known as a hornwork. This arrangement is paralleled locally at

Above: A bronze belt-link from the pre-Roman period, found at Old Sarum in 1913 and now in the Salisbury and South Wiltshire Museum
Below: A reconstruction suggesting the appearance of the Iron Age hillfort around 100 BC

Facing page: Tournai marble tomb slab of Bishop Roger (d. 1139) in Salisbury Cathedral, one of the three bishops' tombs moved to the new cathedral on 14 June 1226. The head is thought to have been restored in the later Middle Ages

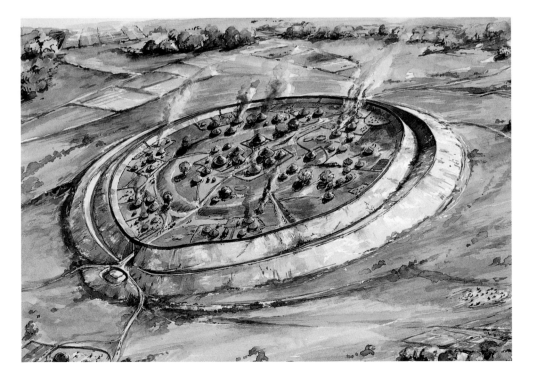

Top: The Iron Age hillfort at Yarnbury Castle. The outline of an earlier enclosure can be seen within the later ramparts. As at Old Sarum, the hillfort developed with a single gate (left), protected by an outer bank or hornwork

Above: Part of the ramparts of Figsbury Ring, which like Old Sarum looks out over the valley of the River Avon

Yarnbury Castle, some 13km (8 miles) north-west of Old Sarum. Here, an early fort of perhaps the sixth century BC was enlarged when a rampart with a single entrance and hornwork was constructed, in the fourth century BC. Whether Old Sarum developed similarly from an earlier and smaller enclosure is impossible to say. However, the finds excavated in 1909–15 and in 1957 suggest that the outer ramparts were built during the Middle Iron Age, perhaps about 400 BC, and so must be more or less contemporary with the enlarged Yarnbury.

Iron Age hillforts had many functions, acting as markets, storehouses, industrial centres and even religious sites. They also served as protective enclosures to which the local population, with their livestock, could retreat in times of danger. In the Middle and Late Iron Age (between the fourth century BC and first century AD), some were permanently occupied. Relatively few Iron Age hillforts have been extensively excavated, but of those that have, Danebury (Hampshire) and Maiden Castle stand out as being so successful as settlements that they dominated their local economies and might even be thought of as early towns.

Unfortunately, very little evidence has been found of Iron Age occupation of Old Sarum. In 1913, rubbish pits containing pre-Roman pottery and a bronze belt-link were found on the site of the later cathedral nave; these probably date from the first century BC. Evidence of occupation of a broadly similar date was uncovered in 1957 around the north-eastern sector of the rampart. Old Sarum's location, however, suggests that in its early history the hillfort served as a refuge and market centre. Sited on a promontory, and backing on to cultivated fields and pasture, it was perfectly situated to overlook the natural resources – game, fish, fruit, reed and timber – of the river valley below.

ROMAN OCCUPATION

It is during the Roman period that Old Sarum begins to appear in documentary records, as Sorviodunum. According to the Antonine Itinerary (a late Roman description of the road network), it lay 20 Roman miles from Venta Belgarum (Winchester) and on the road to Isca Dumniorum (Exeter). In fact, three Roman roads from the north and east converged outside the east gate of the hillfort, from Winchester, London (via Silchester) and Cirencester (via Mildenhall). Of these the middle road became known as the Portway, and it continued south-west, crossing the Avon beyond modern Stratford-sub-Castle and emerging on the far side of the Nadder, where it is known as Ackling Dyke. From there it ran to Durnovaria (Dorchester) and Exeter.

The pre-medieval levels of the hillfort have never been systematically excavated, so what is known of Roman Sorviodunum is limited. Nevertheless, the 1957 excavations showed that the hillfort was continuously occupied between the Roman conquest (AD 43) and the early fourth century. Moreover, while investigating an unfinished medieval well within the inner bailey in 1911, archaeologists discovered the original Iron Age ground level, 5.2m (17ft) below that of the Norman earthworks. When the excavators dug two horizontal galleries at this level, they found Romano-British occupation layers 90cm (3ft) thick, and two sections of wall with a flint core, forming the corner of a building. The internal pavement of this building sealed an Iron Age pit, suggesting that it is likely to be Roman.

Above: A Romano-British bronze brooch, dating from the first century AD and found at Old Sarum. It is now in the Salisbury and South Wiltshire Museum

Below: An early medieval whistle pipe, carved from a small bone, found at Old Sarum and also now in the museum at Salisbury

We know much more about Roman life outside the line of the ramparts, where two sizeable Romano-British settlements have been identified. One of these was 400–500m (440–550yds) south-east of the east entrance to the hillfort, close to where the north end of the Paul's Dene housing estate now lies. This settlement was established by the late first century AD, but flourished during the fourth century, when occupation of the hillfort seems to have been in decline. The second was a substantial roadside settlement, straddling the Portway, and extending from a point around 500m (550yds) south-west of the east gate through Stratford-sub-Castle almost as far as the Roman river crossing of the Avon.

One way of interpreting this evidence is to see the hillfort as having a specific purpose. It has even been suggested that the walls uncovered beneath the inner bailey belonged to a Romano-British temple and that here, as at South Cadbury (Somerset), an Iron Age hillfort was adopted as a religious centre. It is equally likely that in the early Roman period a military fort would have been set up within the earthworks. If so, a *vicus*, or civilian settlement, would have been established outside the ramparts, which formed the nucleus of one, or both, of the extra-mural Roman settlements. The latter clearly

Right: Map of the area around
Old Sarum, showing rivers,
neighbouring Iron Age fortifications
and Roman roads

Below: This gold ring, bearing the
name of King Ethelwulf of Wessex
(reigned 839–58), was found
near Old Sarum. It is now in the
British Museum

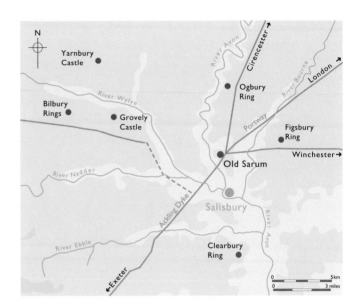

flourished, and their importance as local market centres was
assured by their position on the road network. During the
later Roman period, the old earthworks could still be
occupied in times of distress – for instance, when invasion
was threatened, or during periods of local warfare. But by
the fourth century it seems that the social and economic
importance of the extra-mural settlements had become
much greater than that of the old hillfort.

ANGLO-SAXON OLD SARUM

No evidence has so far come to light to determine the fate
of Sorviodunum at the end of the Roman period, though
it is one of the few post-Roman sites in Wiltshire to be
documented. Under the year 552, the Anglo-Saxon Chronicle
notes: 'In this year Cynric fought against the Britons at the
place called Searobyrg, and put the Britons to flight.' Searobyrg
is the Anglo-Saxon name for Old Sarum. This would suggest
that there was a post-Roman British population in the area in
the mid-sixth century, and that the old hillfort was in use as a
regional centre and stronghold.

    We also know little about Old Sarum during the later
Anglo-Saxon period. A bronze brooch and a few silver
pennies from the reigns of Aethelstan (925–40) and Edgar
(959–75) hint at Old Sarum's use as a defensive refuge during
the tenth century. However, it is Wilton, and not Old Sarum,
which is listed in the early tenth-century Burghal Hidage – a
list of defensible towns in Wessex – and which gave its name
to the county of Wiltshire. In 1003 the Anglo-Saxon Chronicle
records that Sweyn, king of Denmark, destroyed Exeter and
Wilton and 'betook him then to Searobyrg, and from there
went back to the sea'. One result of this attack is that the
mint at Wilton moved to Old Sarum, along with three of the
four Wilton moneyers. The mint would have been sited within

the old hillfort, so occupation must have returned to Old Sarum. Archaeological work has also established that there was late Anglo-Saxon settlement outside the ramparts.

Finally, Domesday Book tells us that before 1066 Old Sarum was considered a borough, which by the date of Domesday was known as Sarisberie, and that it lay towards the centre of a huge estate held by the bishop of Ramsbury and Sherborne. The estate described in Domesday as Sarisberie extended to around 9 square miles, centred on Old Sarum and comprising the land on which modern Salisbury was founded, as well as the later parishes of Milford, Stratford-sub-Castle and Woodford. This estate was certainly vested in the bishop by 1066, and possibly as early as 909. But the seat of the bishop had been unusually peripatetic. Before 908–9 Wiltshire had formed part of the diocese of Winchester, but in the early tenth century an attempt was made to subdivide this enormous diocese, and a new see was created at Ramsbury to cover Wiltshire and Berkshire. The bishops may have been granted Old Sarum either at that point or later. What is certain is that the endowments of the bishops of Ramsbury and their neighbours the bishops of Sherborne were slowly wasted over the next century and a half – so much so that the two dioceses had to be united in 1058. The bishop of Ramsbury and Sherborne then took Sherborne as his principal residence. So, when the diocesan centre was again moved, after the Norman Conquest, to Old Sarum, the see had already been moved twice in the previous 200 years, and the bishops were moving onto part of their own estate.

Above: A gold coin minted at Old Sarum, which may have been paid to the Danes as tribute money or 'Danegeld', as it later found its way to Sweden. It bears the name of King Ethelred (reigned 978–1016)
Below: King William the Conqueror (reigned 1066–87) enthroned, from a 13th-century manuscript

THE NORMAN CASTLE

Whatever kind of settlement already existed at Old Sarum, William the Conqueror recognised its potential as a fortification shortly after the Conquest. Although the exact date at which the new castle was created is uncertain, a charter issued 'in the king's chamber in the castle called Seresberi [Old Sarum]' has been dated to 1069–70. This makes Old Sarum part of a first wave of royal castles built to establish Norman rule after 1066.

A new motte was created in the centre of the old hillfort, and two lateral banks were erected to enclose an outer bailey. Not only could this have been done quickly, but the scale of the outer bailey was sufficient to accommodate a large body of troops (see page 14). Old Sarum's position on the road network may also have recommended the old hillfort as an ideal army base in the early stages of the Norman Conquest. Its importance as an administrative base grew thereafter, as the sheriffs of Wiltshire were established in the castle and the new cathedral was created. This provided a body of literate clerks who are known to have assisted with major administrative projects.

Right: This section of the Bayeux Tapestry shows a motte being constructed layer by layer. A similar practice would have been followed at Old Sarum, where the level of the inner bailey was about 5m (17ft) above the previous (Roman) ground level

Below: A bone chess piece found at Old Sarum, dating from the 12th or 13th century (now in the Salisbury and South Wiltshire Museum)

All early buildings in the castle would have been of timber, and it is likely that the keep was the first structure to be built in stone, probably early in the reign of Henry I (1100–35). The earliest documentary reference to the building is in 1130, when the sheriff spent 20 shillings 'making a doorway to the cellar of the tower'. It must have been shortly after this that Bishop Roger of Sarum obtained the castle, 'which properly belonged to the king' as William of Malmesbury put it. Roger's work on the castle is largely undocumented, but the case for attributing the courtyard house to him is strong.

Roger already had a bishop's palace to the north of the cathedral, so at first sight building another house within the castle might seem something of an overprovision. However, medieval magnates were very conscious of the roles to which they aspired. Roger had to have a bishop's palace: it was where he discharged his duties, both symbolically and practically, as a model bishop living in the midst of the cathedral community – a kind of official residence. But by the early 1120s Roger was also widely recognised as Henry I's chief minister, and was regent during Henry's absences abroad. The courtyard house was almost certainly intended to give architectural expression to this role, and provide for Roger in his position as the king's deputy. In this sense it was surplus neither to the bishop's palace, nor to the keep, even though it duplicated some of the accommodation in both – it simply arose out of Roger's particular circumstances. His downfall in 1139 (see page 8) and the subsequent return of the castle to the king brought to an end the period of ambitious, if idiosyncratic, building at Old Sarum.

THE CASTLE AND THE PLANTAGENETS

The castle then seems to have passed on to a cycle of routine care and maintenance, unbroken until Henry II began to make modest improvements in the 1170s. Between 1171 and 1189 over £300 was spent on the castle. The gatehouse was refurbished and a new drawbridge built; the inner bailey was surrounded by a masonry wall; and a treasury was

constructed in the keep. This work broadly coincides with the period in which Henry was lavishing a colossal amount of money on his great hunting palace at nearby Clarendon, and reflects a renewed royal interest in Old Sarum.

Some of the money is likely to have been spent on the repair or refurbishment of quarters for the queen, Eleanor of Aquitaine, who seems to have been kept under house arrest at Old Sarum for most of the 1170s. She was arrested for having incited her sons to rebel against their father, Henry II, in 1173, and spent the next 16 years in detention. The Limousin chronicler Geoffrey de Vigeois maintains that for much of this time she was held at Old Sarum. It appears that she was kept in some comfort here: between 1175 and 1180 large amounts of money were spent by the sheriff of Wiltshire on the queen's maintenance, and fine clothes for Eleanor and her household seem to have been regularly despatched from London.

The castle continued to be kept in good repair during the reigns of Richard I (1189–99) and John (1199–1216), and a new hall, kitchen and bakehouse were created for the sheriff between 1201 and 1208. However, the latter stages of John's reign were marked by a sharp deterioration in relations with the cathedral clergy. It was probably at this period that the old side passage beside the keep, which provided easy access to the cathedral, was blocked up. The limitations of Old Sarum as an administrative centre began to bite. The abandonment of Old Sarum by the clergy during the 1220s marked the end of serious royal interest in the castle; and it is as a rather grand sheriff's office that the later medieval castle is best understood.

Above: The tomb effigy of Eleanor of Aquitaine (d. 1204), Henry II's queen, at the abbey of Fontevraud, France. Eleanor was kept a virtual prisoner by her husband for 16 years, and probably spent much of this time at Old Sarum
Below: The inner bailey of the medieval castle at Old Sarum, viewed from the south-west

THE FIRST CATHEDRAL

The first cathedral was created after the 1075 Council of London decreed that the see should be moved from Sherborne to Old Sarum. According to William of Malmesbury, Herman (bishop of Ramsbury from 1045 and of the united sees of Sherborne and Ramsbury from 1058) began work on the new cathedral; but he was already an old man, and when he died, in 1078, work had not proceeded far. His successor, Osmund (1078–99), is described as the builder of the cathedral in the 1091 foundation charter, and it was Osmund who shaped the character and constitution of Old Sarum Cathedral.

The choice of Old Sarum was probably motivated by a combination of its position within one of the bishop's manors, and its proximity to a royal castle. It was not, however, an obvious location for a bishopric as were Chichester, Exeter, Norwich or Lincoln – all of which became new diocesan centres between 1050 and 1100, and all of which were substantial towns. At Old Sarum it is not clear whether the mid-11th-century population exceeded that of Wilton (then the county town of Wiltshire), let alone Sherborne; and on balance it seems likely that Old Sarum was chosen because it suited the royal administration. Before his appointment as bishop, Osmund had served as royal chancellor (1070–78), and may even have played a role in the decision to move the see.

Most of what is known about the type of community that served the first cathedral comes from Osmund's charter of 1091. This records the endowment necessary to support the work of the cathedral chapter – six manors and 21 parish churches – mostly drawn from Osmund's own episcopal estates; and states that the bishop 'has established canons in the church', who were living according to a rule. The canons, or priests, were probably in residence in 1089, when the annals of Holyrood state that Osmund had introduced 36 canons at Old Sarum.

Above: Initial 'A' from a manuscript copy of Aldhelm's In Praise of Virginity, acquired by Osmund for the library at Old Sarum while he was bishop. St Aldhelm was the founding bishop of Sherborne, who died in 709

Right: The Purbeck marble tomb shrine of St Osmund in Salisbury Cathedral. This may have been made around 1180 for the east chapel at Old Sarum. The holes, known as foramina, were for the use of pilgrims, who would kneel forward in prayer, placing their heads and hands inside them

Less is known about the chapter before this, though a group of priests must already have been resident at Old Sarum, who not only formed the basis of the bishop's household, but created a remarkable collection of manuscripts. William of Malmesbury tells us that Osmund drew around himself a community of scribes and scholars, and a study of manuscripts produced at Old Sarum has revealed that 17 different scribes were active there before Osmund's death in 1099. Three of them helped to draw up the Exon Domesday of 1086, the draft survey of landholding for south-western England, which suggests that relations between the royal administration in the castle and the early cathedral community were close.

We cannot be sure where either the scriptorium, in which the manuscripts were produced, or the early canons' residences were sited. It is clear, however, that the cathedral church consecrated under Osmund was part of a larger precinct, and that the first bishop's palace was created during this period.

Below: A page from the Decretals *of* Pseudo-Isidore, *one of a remarkable group of manuscripts produced at Old Sarum while Osmund was bishop. The margins were annotated with the letters DM (dignum memoria, or 'worthy of memory') by a scribe or scholar who added similar notes to 25 surviving books from Old Sarum*

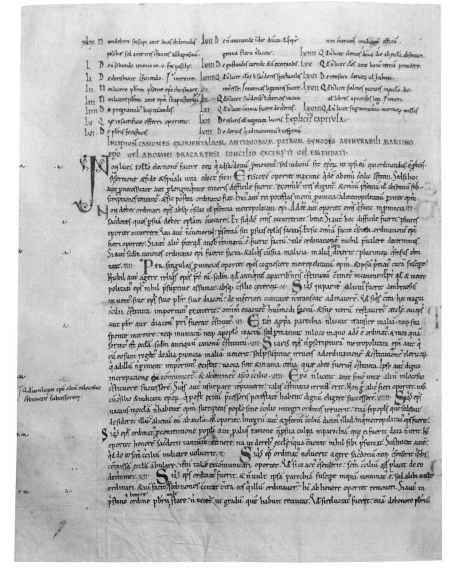

Right: Carved heads discovered in a storage pit near the south transept in 1912. The heads probably embellished the exterior of Roger's new presbytery
Below: Stone coffin-lid with an inscription celebrating Godwin, precentor of Old Sarum in the early 12th century, and explaining that before he came to Old Sarum he had been a priest under Archbishop Anselm at Canterbury. The tomb was one of over 20 discovered in 1912–13 in the canons' cemetery

ROGER AND THE SECOND CATHEDRAL

It was under Bishops Roger (1102–39) and Jocelyn de Bohun (1142–84) that the constitution of Old Sarum took on the character by which it was known for the rest of the Middle Ages. The rule by which Osmund's chapter of canons lived is unclear. Their endowment provided for a common fund, which seems to suggest that they lived communally like monks, and would therefore have required a refectory (dining hall) and dormitory. However, we are told that while Roger was bishop some canons had houses and gardens outside the gate of Old Sarum. Around 1120, the cathedral's first precentor (choir master), Godwin, even argued that canons might be allowed to own land privately without contravening the rule under which they lived, provided they used their resources for the needs of the church. This seems perfectly to capture the sort of semi-independent community that came into being at Old Sarum in the early 12th century.

The system of farming chapter estates to provide for the entire community had given way by about 1150 to one in which each canon had a particular piece of land and parish church, known as a prebend, which provided his income. Nevertheless, a portion of the estate was reserved to provide a communal fund, so that canons who assisted at cathedral services would receive a daily allowance, their 'commons', over and above any prebendal income. Over this same period, the 'four-square' hierarchy of cathedral officers also evolved, with the dean as head of the chapter, a precentor in charge of the choir, a treasurer in charge of church ornaments and a chancellor in charge of readings in church and education. This arrangement of officials was eventually codified as the Use of Sarum, and became the model for the chapters of all other English secular (non-monastic) cathedrals in the later Middle Ages.

All this required space, and it is surprising that, although Roger seems to have built a new palace beside his cathedral for the bishop and his household early in his episcopacy, work on extending the cathedral seems to have waited until about 1130. Other than the plan, evidence for this new work is fragmentary, though the extraordinary quality and variety of geometric sculpture that survives suggest that it was the most extravagant and ornamentally detailed building of its day. William of Malmesbury gives a vivid impression of the effect

it had on contemporaries: 'at Salisbury [Old Sarum] and Malmesbury he [Roger] erected buildings large in scale, expensive and very beautiful to look at – the courses of stone being laid so exactly that the joints defy inspection and give the whole wall the appearance of a single rock-face. Salisbury [Old Sarum] cathedral he rebuilt and richly furnished, so that it is passed by no church in England and surpasses many, and he himself can say to God with perfect truth – "Lord, I have loved the beauty of Thy house".'

Roger never lived to see his cathedral completed. The later work at Old Sarum was done under his successor, Jocelyn de Bohun, who fitted out Roger's new east end, abandoned the idea of replacing the nave, and added a new twin-towered west front as a finishing touch. During Jocelyn's episcopacy the first miracles before the tomb of Osmund are reported, and it is likely that the axial eastern chapel was refurbished in response and that Osmund's remains were translated to a shrine-tomb there in about 1180.

The layout and position of the cloister suggest that it too must have been commissioned by Jocelyn. This is curious, as by this date it was becoming common for the cathedral chapter to be non-resident. Perhaps it was intended to remind the canons of their duties and communal roots.

Above: Carved animal mask from the nave at Malmesbury Abbey, one of a handful of locations where Old Sarum sculptors also worked. The distinctive cutting of the eyes is almost identical to that of some of the carved heads from Old Sarum (see opposite and page 1)

Below: A reconstruction of Roger's new cathedral viewed from the south-east, with the canons' cemetery and cemetery cross in the foreground

Above: A capital from the south-east transept at Salisbury Cathedral depicting Bishop Richard Poore, who engineered the move to Salisbury (New Sarum)

Below: Salisbury from Old Sarum by J M W Turner, painted in about 1828–9. Many artists of the Romantic movement were to recognise the picturesque qualities of both new and old cities

THE MOVE TO NEW SARUM

One of the milestones in the history of Old Sarum was the decision by the clergy to abandon the cathedral in favour of a new site in the valley below. Although it was not until 1220 that Bishop Richard Poore (1217–28) organised the ceremonial laying of foundation stones for a new cathedral, dissatisfaction with the old site can be traced back some 30 years. Indeed, royal approval for the move was given as early as 1194. A papal bull issued in 1218 gives a list of reasons why the clergy wanted to move. Accommodation was in such short supply that the canons had to rent houses from the laity. Water was scarce, and had to be bought at a high price; the fabric of the cathedral was so ruinous that it was 'a constant danger to the congregation'; and the site was so windy that 'those celebrating the divine offices can hardly hear each other speak'.

Relations with the castle garrison had also deteriorated. A low was reached in 1217 when the dean and clergy of Old Sarum returned from a procession to St Martin's Church at Milford and were refused entry through the east gate. These complaints clearly rankled, but the chapter was probably being pulled as well as pushed. The main centres of population were almost certainly outside the ramparts by this date, closer to the Avon at Milford, and the bishop was as much following his flock as leading them when it came to creating a new city.

Nonetheless, the move was brilliantly executed, and it was designed to suggest that the new cathedral was continuous with the old. Not only was New Sarum (Salisbury) Cathedral planned to accommodate the Old Sarum liturgy, but it was also to house its former bishops, and even make use of its stones.

The Demolition of the Cathedral

On 14 June 1226, the tombs of Osmund, Roger and Jocelyn were moved to the new cathedral, and the demolition of the old cathedral could begin. The parapet walls of the new presbytery at Salisbury Cathedral were begun in 1227, and are lined with re-used stone from Old Sarum. From this date until perhaps the 1260s, it seems likely that stone was regularly carried the 3km (2 miles) between the two sites. On arrival at Salisbury it was used not only to line the gallery and upper walls of the new cathedral, but also in the close wall and south cloister walk.

Excavations in 1913 uncovered evidence of how Old Sarum Cathedral was demolished. William St John Hope, who directed the excavations, reported discovering two sections of wall where it was obvious that large cavities had been cut in the masonry and props of wood inserted, which were then set on fire: 'as they burnt the walling above subsided into the hollows in fractured masses or was overthrown in bulk'. The materials would then have been sorted, and squared stone, even if it was decorated with simple geometric motifs, was cleaned and put aside for re-use. In 1912, masses of stone chippings, pits containing some of the best surviving Romanesque sculpture, and a limekiln were found near the south transept: this suggests that irregularly shaped stones were piled up before being burned to make lime. Some of the best sculpture recovered during excavation is now on display at the Salisbury and South Wiltshire Museum.

Stone was regularly carried between Old Sarum and the new cathedral at Salisbury, where much of it was re-used

Above: Detail of the wall of the cathedral close in Salisbury (top), and a vault pocket in the roof above the north-east transept of the cathedral. Both were faced with stone re-used from Old Sarum
Left: Loose stone from Old Sarum, stacked during the excavations in 1910

FROM CITY TO ROTTEN BOROUGH

Although the relocation of the cathedral in the 1220s did not deprive Old Sarum of all purpose, the difference between Roger's Old Sarum in the 1130s and the situation a century later is stark. By 1240, half the outer bailey was in ruins, the castle was in need of major repairs, and the vast majority of the local population lived in New Sarum (Salisbury) or the suburbs, outside the Iron Age ramparts. The removal of the cathedral to Salisbury had finally crystallised a problem inherent from the outset: Old Sarum was an unsuitable location for a town.

Nonetheless, life continued within the ramparts, mostly in the castle, although with the cathedral now gone, technically the whole area within the ramparts belonged to the castle. The final clearance of the cathedral precinct probably took place in 1331, when the dean and chapter were granted the remaining materials for use in fortifying the wall of the cathedral close at Salisbury. One rather curious structure did remain in good repair until the 16th century – a chantry chapel, where prayers were offered for the souls of the dead – which the chapter were bound to rebuild in 1332.

The castle within the inner bailey continued in use throughout the 13th and 14th centuries. Over £700 was spent on its repair and maintenance during the reign of Edward III (1327–77). Although the 1315 estimate for the cost of repairs to the keep was £600, the money was not spent, which suggests that some of the structures in the inner bailey must have been abandoned. The most extensive repairs were made to the courtyard house, which was identified in 1330 as the building 'in which the sheriff and his officers dwell' and which was the subject of a major overhaul in 1366. The castle seems to have tottered on as an administrative centre

Below: An engraving of Old Sarum and Salisbury made in 1723 by the antiquarian William Stukeley

The Reformers' Attack on the Old Rotten Tree; or, the Foul Nests of the Cormorants in Danger.

Left: A caricature showing those for and against the Reform Bill of 1832, depicting the outdated electoral system as a rotten tree. Old Sarum, which appears on one of the lower left branches, was often cited as one of the most notorious 'rotten boroughs', which did not have any real voters

Below: A sketch dating from about 1700 showing the Old Sarum 'burgage plots'. At election time, the landowner granted short leases on two narrow plots (just above centre, to the right of the main road) adjoining the 'Parliament Tree'; the leaseholders voted for the owner's nominee, and then relinquished their leases

into the 15th century. The end finally came in 1514, when Henry VIII made over the 'stones called the castle or tower of Old Sarum' to Thomas Compton, one of his officials, together with the right to carry away the materials.

Far less is known about the outer bailey and suburbs. The 1377 poll tax returns list 3,226 taxpayers in Salisbury and only ten in Old Sarum, suggesting that the latter could no longer be considered a town. The east gate itself was maintained at a cost to the king, and repairs were made to its upper chapel as late as the late 1440s; but, by the time the antiquarian John Leland visited Old Sarum in 1540, even the east suburb was no more: 'Ther is not one house [with]in Old Saresbyri or without inhabited.'

These events did not deprive Old Sarum of borough status, however. Despite its lack of population, Old Sarum continued to send members to Parliament from 1360 until the 1832 Great Reform Act formally abolished such 'rotten boroughs', where election results were effectively controlled by the landowner. As Edmund Burke put it in 1780, 'Old Sarum was once a place of trade, now you can only trace the streets by the colour of the corn, and its sole manufacture is in members of parliament.' Traditionally, the borough representatives were elected beneath the 'Parliament Tree', an elm which, until it was cut down in 1905, stood south of the ramparts and close to the line of the Portway (the Roman road to Dorchester).

It is slowly becoming clear that what was understood in the Middle Ages as the borough of Old Sarum was never actually inside the ramparts. The early 13th-century description by Henry of Avranches – 'the city stood in the castle and the castle in the city' – was a poetic fiction. Rather, the medieval 'borough' was actually by the old Parliament Tree, outside the ramparts – what Leland described as 'in time of mynd … a fair suburbe'.

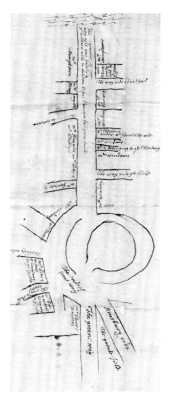

Above: A watercolour view of Old Sarum by John Constable, looking south-west towards the ramparts across Stratford-sub-Castle on a stormy day. The picture was exhibited at the Royal Academy in 1834

OLD SARUM REDISCOVERED

Little is known about Old Sarum between John Leland's visit in 1540 and the early 19th century. Samuel Pepys visited the site in 1668 and was impressed, finding the ramparts 'prodigious so as to affright him to be there alone at night'. The castle and manor of Old Sarum were successively owned by the Cecil earls of Salisbury and the Pitt family: William Pitt the Elder was MP for Old Sarum from 1734 until 1747. But, as Edmund Burke remarked, the value of the site was its parliamentary status. The old hillfort was simply left as pasture and rented out to a sheep farmer.

This began to change in the 19th century. As the Great Reform Act swept away Old Sarum's MP, the Romantic movement ensured that the site's picturesque qualities were recognised, and both Turner and Constable exhibited paintings of Old Sarum at the Royal Academy. Antiquarian interest was also stimulated by the appearance during the exceptionally dry summer of 1834 of scorch marks, indicating the foundations of the cathedral. This prompted Henry Hatcher, a local historian, to produce the first account of the former cathedral's likely plan.

Serious archaeology had to wait until 1909, however, when the Society of Antiquaries of London obtained permission to excavate the site. Lieutenant-Colonel William Hawley was put in charge of day-to-day operations, with D. H. Montgomerie as site surveyor, draughtsman and photographer; Sir William St John Hope, a distinguished architectural historian and antiquary, oversaw operations from London. Hope would generally visit the excavations four or five times a season, and was the principal interpreter of what was found, presenting interim reports in the form of lectures to the Society of Antiquaries.

Beneath the Ramparts

David Algar and David Truckle remember the 1957 excavations:

'As young members of the Salisbury Field Club we were given the rare opportunity in November 1957 to help with an excavation at Old Sarum. Under the direction of Philip Rahtz, a trench was laid inside the northern rampart in the hope of finding a tunnel, thought to be medieval, which had first been revealed in 1795.

'After several days of shovelling, the co-director of the work, John Musty, was probing the bottom of the trench when the steel rod he was pushing on suddenly disappeared into the ground and he fell flat. A hole about 6 inches in diameter appeared. Peering into this with a torch revealed a void. As the suspense grew the trench was widened for safety reasons before work could proceed. Looking back at the photographs now, one is amazed at the complete lack of safety helmets and minimal shuttering. One block fell out of the roof during the time we were in there. However, we all survived, most having taken the opportunity to do some "caving".

'The chalk-cut tunnel was a splendid construction, with a fine arched roof and neatly finished walls still showing the tool marks of the builders. The immediate impression was one of unexpected space – it was possible to stand upright about 20 feet from the entrance. The interior was quite dry and rather dusty. You got out by scrambling up the steep consolidated scree, pulling yourself up a fixed rope. The walls bore the names and initials of early 19th-century visitors, some scratched into the chalk or written in crayon or lamp black from lighted candles. We remember the names Sidford, Gilbert, Crouch and Archer. The last was taken up by a news headline writer: "The Archers were there".'

> 'Looking back now, one is amazed at the complete lack of safety helmets and minimal shuttering'

Left: Members of the Royal Commission on Historical Monuments Salisbury office investigating the tunnel beneath the ramparts in 1957

The problems presented by the site were formidable. In the first place, anything between 1.2 and 3m (4–10ft) of soil and debris had to be removed before foundation walls were revealed, and elaborate tramways were constructed to carry away the spoil. The spoil heap from the castle now forms the platform on which the car park sits. Spoil from the cathedral was tipped over the northern ramparts. Secondly, much of the site, the cathedral in particular, had been so completely robbed of stone that interpretation of the findings was problematic. Even the plan of Roger's cathedral remains a matter of dispute. Thirdly, the excavations were interrupted by the First World War. Between 1909 and 1911 Hawley and Hope had concentrated on the castle, whose ruins were then consolidated in 1912. Between 1912 and 1915 they focused on the cathedral, but the 1915 season was short and hurried. With the First World War entering a second year, Hawley found it almost impossible to get labourers.

Hope's report of these operations expressed optimism that the Society of Antiquaries would be able to complete the excavations eventually, and that a proper account of the finds, and particularly of the stonework, would be published. But it was not to be. Hope died in 1919, and though Hawley's field diaries survive, only rarely do they record where loose stone was found. The absence of an accurate record of the stone finds hampers our ability to understand the complexities of Old Sarum Cathedral.

These excavations were the last on a genuinely grand scale. Recent work has been more limited, focusing on the ramparts, the site of the Second World War pillbox (see page 21), or the areas immediately outside the old hillfort. However, less can be more. Modern archaeology has become adept at extracting information from often very small digs. Moreover, remote sensing techniques are now developing so rapidly that another century from now our understanding of Old Sarum is likely to be much fuller than it is today.